Awful ANIMAL PHOBIAS

by John Wood &
Noah Leatherland

BEARPORT
PUBLISHING

Minneapolis, Minnesota

Credits

Images are courtesy of Shutterstock.com. With thanks to Getty Images, Thinkstock Photo, and iStockphoto. RECURRING – pikepicture, kantimar kongjaidee, MagicMary. COVER – SpicyTruffel, Chanawat Jaiya, KittyVector, Svetsol, Vera Larina, Dalhazz, julio chaniago 76, Magicleaf, podtin. 4–5 – maxim ibragimov, sicegame, Krakenimages.com. 7 – Kurit afshen, SpicyTruffel. 8–9 – Calvin Ang, Muangsatun, Kert, VectorShow. 10–11 – Studio 37, pirita, VectorPlotnikoff. 12–13 – Giovanni Cancemi, OlegRi. 14–15 – Sergey Uryadnikov, Willyam Bradberry, Gaslop. 16–17 – Scott E Read, oksana2010, Simply Amazing. 18–19 – Adwo, isarescheewin, Edge Creative. 20–21 – M Rose, Nadya_Art, Unknown Author, Public domain, via Wikimedia Commons. 22–23 – GOLFWORA, jekjob, LinaOro. 24–25 – Fehmiu Roffytavare, Fehmiu Roffytavare, Svetsol. 26–27 – Eric Isselee, Contes de fee, TigerStocks. 28–29 – clickit, Rudmer Zwerver, Photoongraphy.

Bearport Publishing Company Product Development Team

President: Jen Jenson; Director of Product Development: Spencer Brinker; Managing Editor: Allison Juda; Associate Editor: Naomi Reich; Associate Editor: Tiana Tran; Art Director: Colin O'Dea; Designer: Elena Klinkner; Designer: Kayla Eggert; Product Development Assistant: Owen Hamlin

Library of Congress Cataloging-in-Publication Data

Names: Wood, John, 1990- author. | Leatherland, Noah, 1999- author.
Title: Awful animal phobias / by John Wood & Noah Leatherland.
Description: Roar! books. | Minneapolis, Minnesota : Bearport Publishing Company, [2024] | Series: Circus of fears | Includes bibliographical references and index.
Identifiers: LCCN 2023037697 (print) | LCCN 2023037698 (ebook) | ISBN 9798889166122 (library binding) | ISBN 9798889166177 (paperback) | ISBN 9798889166214 (ebook)
Subjects: LCSH: Animal phobias--Juvenile literature. | Fear--Juvenile literature.
Classification: LCC RC552.A48 W66 2024 (print) | LCC RC552.A48 (ebook) | DDC 616.85/225--dc23/eng/20230821
LC record available at https://lccn.loc.gov/2023037697
LC ebook record available at https://lccn.loc.gov/2023037698

For more information, write to Bearport Publishing, 5357 Penn Avenue South, Minneapolis, MN 55419.

CONTENTS

WELCOME
★ TO THE ★
SHOW!

> COME ONE, COME ALL! SEE THE AMAZING CIRCUS OF FEARS!

Everyone is afraid of something. But do you have a phobia? This is a very strong fear. You may even have a phobia of something that cannot cause you any real danger.

> People have phobias of all sorts of things. Some common phobias are of spiders and flying on planes.

Our circus is all about real fears. Are you ready to find out what scares people the most?

Maybe you will leave the show with a brand-new phobia of your own. . . .

THE SCIENCE ★ OF ★ FEAR

First, let's find out more about fear. Your body has three **responses** when you are scared.

FIGHT

You feel angry, and your muscles tense up. You are ready to battle.

FLIGHT

Your heart beats faster, and your breathing speeds up. You are ready to run away.

FREEZE

You feel as if you can't move or think. Scientists say your body may be trying to play dead.

These responses help when there is a threat. But sometimes your body and brain get confused about what is dangerous. A phobia might make your body respond to something that can't hurt you.

Some people have phobias of horses.

Let's learn more about some phobias of awful animals!

★ SCARY ★
SNAKES

What is it about snakes that people find so scary? Is it the way they **slither** across the ground? Maybe it is how they quickly jump at their **prey**.

Some people may be afraid of how snakes look. They are covered in scales. Snakes have sharp fangs, forked tongues, and beady eyes.

Some snakes really are dangerous. They can **inject** an animal (even a person) with deadly **venom**.

Most snakes leave humans alone, unless people get too close. But that doesn't stop a lot of people from being afraid of them!

★ ICKY ★ INSECTS

Sometimes, even very small things can be scary! How do you feel about bugs?

There are lots of bugs in the world. In fact, there are about 1.4 billion insects for every person on Earth! That's a whole lot of buzzing, clicking, and crawling.

What is it about insects that bothers people? Some do not like the bugs' three body parts, six legs, and **antennae**. Others are scared of the way they move.

Some people are afraid of only some kinds of insects, such as cockroaches. To be honest, these insects probably bug most of us!

HORRID HORSES

Many people love horses. However, there are some who find them terrifying!

Horses are large and powerful animals. They can be taller than adult humans and carry hundreds of pounds.

Some horses are well behaved. But others can be a bit more difficult! A horse's kick can be dangerous.

People with a phobia of horses might also be scared of other animals with hooves, such as donkeys and mules.

SHARK ATTACK

The sight of a **dorsal** fin sticking out of the water can make anyone shiver. It means there is a shark in the darkness below!

There are more than 500 kinds of sharks. That's plenty to be afraid of. While some of these feared fish are small and harmless, many are not. They are some of the top **predators** in Earth's oceans.

Sharks have rows and rows of teeth that make them perfect hunters. When one tooth falls out, another moves forward to take its place.

Luckily, sharks rarely bite humans. There are fewer than 100 people a year who truly face this fear.

FRIGHTFUL FUR ★

Fear of animals with sharp claws and terrible teeth might keep you from heading to the woods. Those would scare anybody.

But for some people, there is something even more frightening. For those with a certain phobia, there is nothing scarier than an animal's fur or skin.

The feel of fur can cause this phobia. Others shiver at the thought of the bugs and germs in that fur.

People with this phobia will even stay away from furry pets, such as cats and dogs. Some may avoid clothes made from fur!

ROTTEN RATS

Some small, squeaky animals terrify lots of people. These critters crawl. They eat garbage at night. What are they? Rats!

Rats can carry all sorts of diseases. These little animals have caused millions of deaths throughout history.

People with a phobia of rats might worry about getting sick. Or they may simply hate the way rats look.

Even those who do not mind rats might fear the rat king! Some people believe this happens when several rats get their tails tangled. They form a single ball of wriggling creatures. *Yikes!*

SHOCKING SHELLS

Shellfish are sea creatures with shells. Shrimp, crabs, lobsters, and clams are all types of shellfish. These animals are some of the strangest creatures below the waves.

We don't often see shellfish. They live in deep parts of the sea, swimming and crawling in search of food.

Shellfish may look spiky, rough, slimy, or gooey. Some have sharp **pincers**, spiky shells, or long antennae.

For a person with this phobia, just the thought of these odd underwater creatures causes panic. They can't even stand to see videos or photos of shellfish!

★ FARM ★ FEAR

Which small farm animal bobs its head, clucks, and pecks at the dirt? A chicken, of course. Are you afraid?

Some people have a very strong fear of these common birds. Maybe it's because of their sharp beaks and claws. Chickens also have little, black eyes and thin, scaly legs.

No matter the reason, people who have a chicken phobia do everything to avoid them. Strangely, people with chicken phobias are not usually afraid of other birds or animals.

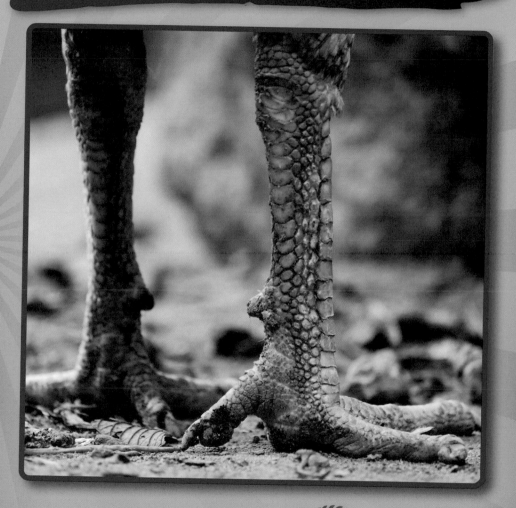

Chickens, like all birds, **evolved** from dinosaurs. Now, that might be a reason to be afraid!

TARANTULA TERROR ★

Which feared creatures have eight legs and usually just as many eyes staring at you? Spiders! These creepy crawlers give plenty of people chills. And tarantulas are some of the scariest!

Tarantulas are large, hairy spiders. There are more than 900 kinds found all around the world. When scared, tarantulas lift their front legs and show their fangs!

Tarantulas are not deadly to humans. Although they have venom in their fangs, they mostly use it to hunt small animals, such as mice.

Scientists have an unusual way to treat someone with a spider phobia. They let the person hold a tarantula! These spiders are usually very calm. When someone gets used to them, their phobia can disappear.

Genghis Khan was born in Mongolia in 1162. He became one of the most powerful warriors in history.

Genghis Khan formed an **empire** that stretched across Asia. His armies were very strong and feared by many people.

What would a powerful leader like Genghis have to be afraid of?

As it turns out, he had a phobia of dogs. To be fair, the dogs in Mongolia at this time in history were big and strong. Maybe that's why Genghis called his **generals** his dogs of war.

27

AFRAID
★ OF ★
ANIMALS

That is the end of our circus of fears! How do you feel? Did you discover a new phobia?

Phobias may be more common than you think. If you've found out you have one, don't worry. People with phobias can get help.

Talk to a trusted adult to learn how. And always remember, the only thing you may have to fear is fear itself!

CURTAIN CLOSE ★

> THANKS FOR COMING! WE HOPE YOU'VE ENJOYED EXPLORING ANIMAL PHOBIAS. COME BACK SOON!

Stay brave for the next time you are forced to face your fears!

GLOSSARY

antennae long, thin body parts that come out of the heads of insects

dorsal the top fin on the back of fish, including sharks

empire a large area of land under one ruler

evolved changed into something else over time

generals people who lead armies

inject to force a liquid into something

pincers pairs of claws that grip things

predators animals that hunt and eat other animals

prey animals that are eaten by other animals

responses reactions

slither to move by sliding back and forth

venom a harmful poison that's injected into the body through a bite or sting

INDEX

Read More

Gunasekara, Mignonne. *Death by Atrocious Animals (Disastrous Deaths).* Minneapolis: Bearport Publishing, 2022.

Spalding, Maddie. *Understanding Phobias (Mental Health Guides).* San Diego: BrightPoint Press, 2022.

Learn More Online

1. Go to **www.factsurfer.com** or scan the QR code below.

2. Enter "**Animal Phobias**" into the search box.

3. Click on the cover of this book to see a list of websites.